Stand By Me

Phyllis Bertin

with

Erin McNiven and Sophia Schwatka

Illustrations by Noel Tuazon

Creative Design by Elizabeth McGoldrick

PAF READING PROGRAM

Pals
Fun in the Sun
Let's Go
Camp Hilltop
Stand By Me
Are We There Yet?

More to come...

Copyright © 2018 by Intelexia USA, LLC.
All rights reserved. No portion of this book may be reproduced in any form without permission from the publisher, except as permitted by U.S. copyright law. For permissions contact: info@PAFprogram.com

Authors: *Phyllis Bertin with Erin McNiven and Sophia Schwatka*
Creative Director: *Elizabeth McGoldrick*
Illustrator: *Noel Tuazon*
ISBN 978-0-9636471-4-6
Printed: *May 2019*
Edition: *May 2019*

pafprogram.com

Fall

1

Ben Hopkins had the jitters. Today he was going to a big picnic with his mom. He was going to see all his pals at the picnic.

It was the end of summer. Ben had missed his pals. They were at camp for the summer. He had wanted to go to camp with his best pal, Nick. Camp cost a lot, so his mom did not let him go.

"Mom, let's get going!" Ben said with a yell.

"I can see you're in a rush," Mrs. Hopkins said.

"Give me a hand with the dishes and then we can go to the picnic."

Ben went to the sink to help his mom. "Will Nick be at the picnic?" he asked.

"Yes," said Mrs. Hopkins. "I asked his mom. She said that Nick wants to see you."

Ben felt very happy. "Good," he said. "I want to see him. He was at camp for so long and I missed him so much."

"Yes, he was," said Mrs. Hopkins. "I bet he missed you as much as you missed him." Ben handed his mom the last dish. "Thank you for helping me. Are you all set to go?" Mrs. Hopkins asked as she put the last dish on the shelf.

Ben and his mom got on the bus to go to the picnic. As they went, they passed the shops and Ben's school. It was not long until they were at the picnic.

"Mom, I'm going to go look for Nick. I won't be long," Ben said. He dashed to look for Nick by the picnic benches. No Nick. He ran past an egg-toss contest. No Nick. At last, he got to the ticket tent. Nick was under the tent.

"Ben!" Nick said as he ran to his pal. "I missed you! Did you have a fun summer?"

"It was OK," said Ben. "Did you have a lot of fun at camp?"

"Yes, I got to fish and swim, and I pitched a tent all by myself," Nick said. Ben looked sad. "Camp will be better if you can go with me next summer," Nick added.

"Thanks," Ben said. "We'll see."

"Let's get tickets and go to the dunk tank," said Nick. "I want to see who is going to get dunked." Nick and Ben got lots of tickets and ran to the dunk tank.

boy

2

Nick and Ben got to the dunk tank. Mr. Hunter sat on a plank on the top of the tank. Mr. Hunter ran Chester School. A bunch of kids were by the tank. They all wanted to see if Mr. Hunter was going to get dunked.

Nick and Ben handed tickets to the man next to the tank. He said, "Thanks. For your tickets, you get a plastic bucket with six balls. If you hit the red button with a ball, Mr. Hunter will get dunked. Good luck!"

"This is going to be fun," Nick said. He pitched all six balls, but missed. "I wish I had hit the button," he said. "You're up, Ben. Give it all you've got!"

Ben did his best. As he tossed the balls, kids chanted, "Dunk him! Dunk him!" But he missed his last shot by just an inch.

All of a sudden, a big kid went up to the dunk tank with his bucket. The rest of the kids looked at him as he pitched a fastball at the button. He hit it! Mr. Hunter fell and sank to the bottom of the tank.

Mr. Hunter was all wet as he went up the rungs of the ladder back to the plank. "What a good shot! I didn't think you kids were going to dunk me so fast," said Mr. Hunter.

Nick went up to the boy. "Good job!" he said.

"Thanks," said the boy.

"I'm Nick."

"I'm Justin."

"Do you go to Chester School?" asked Nick. "I don't think we have met."

Just then Ben ran up to Nick and Justin. "Hi! I'm Ben," he added. But Justin did not chat with Ben. He just said, "So long, Nick!" and dashed to the ticket tent.

Ben asked, "Who is that boy?" He was thinking it was odd that the boy wanted to chat with Nick, but not with him.

"He is Justin. I think he just got to Chester School. Did you see him pitch? He is very good," said Nick. "He dunked Mr. Hunter."

"Yes, he was a good shot," Ben said.

Nick asked, "What is the plan? What do you want to do next? I want to get a hot dog!"

"OK," said Ben, "Hot dogs plus jumbo bags of chips. Let's do it!"

3

The next day, Ben did not want to get up. At ten, he and his mom were going to the shop to get glasses. It was hard for him to read so his mom said he had to have them.

Ben did not want glasses. What if he looked odd? What if the kids said bad things to him?

Ben looked up at his mom. She had her hands on her hips. "What are you doing in bed?" she asked. "You look glum. Are you OK?"

"Mom, do I have to get glasses?" asked Ben.

Mrs. Hopkins sat on the end of Ben's bed. "Yes, Ben. You do."

"But I don't want to get glasses!" he said. "They are for moms and dads. Kids don't have glasses."

"Lots of kids have glasses, Ben. If you look at the kids in school, I bet a bunch of them do. Your glasses are just for reading, so you don't have to have them on all day. Let's go to Mrs. Glenn's shop and get your glasses," she said.

Mrs. Glenn's shop was next to the school. Ben went to the shelf that had glasses for kids. He put on lots of glasses and looked at himself. He did not think they looked very good. "I look like a bug!" he said.

At last, he put on silver glasses and had a look. They were not so bad. Just as he went to tell his mom that he wanted the silver glasses, Liz Beck and her dad rushed into the shop.

Liz was his pal from school. Liz looked at Ben and gasped, "Ben! You look so good in glasses!"

"Thanks," he said. Ben handed the glasses to his mom thinking to himself, "Glasses aren't so bad after all."

4

Nick and Ben were in the den looking at Nick's camp album. It had shots of Nick and his pals catching fish, pitching tents, and singing in the camp contest. Camp looked like such a blast. "I'll ask Mom if I can go next summer," Ben said.

Mrs. Foss, Nick's mom, was yelling for the boys, so they went to see what she wanted. She was fixing dinner. What a mess! She was banging pots and pans, and the sink was filling up with dishes.

"Boys!" said Mrs. Foss. "Will you help me with the muffins? Add a cup of milk, six eggs, and butter to that dish. After you blend it well, it will be all set to put in the black pan."

The boys did what she asked. It was fun mixing the batter. As the batter got thicker, it was harder to mix. Nick was doing his best.

It was going well until Nick's hand hit a glass of milk that was next to the dish. The glass landed with a thud. It was in bits and Nick was upset.

"I'm not the best helper," he said as he looked at the mess.

"Don't be so hard on yourself," said Mrs. Foss. "It happens to all of us! I think you boys are the best helpers. Let me get the dustpan so I can pick up the bits of glass, and then I will blot up the milk."

After Nick's mom picked up the bits of glass, the kids tested the batter. Next, they put big blobs of it into the muffin pan.

Nick's mom looked at all the pots and pans and dishes as she put things in the sink. "It looks like I left a bit of a mess myself," she said. "But that's OK. We had a lot of fun."

5

"One day left until we go back to school," Ben said to himself. He kicked at his blanket and got up from bed.

Mrs. Hopkins had left for her job. She had put a plastic bag with cash on Ben's desk. Next to it, she left a list of what she wanted him to get done by the end of the day.

On the back of the list it said, "Have a good day, Ben! I'll be back by one." Ben looked at the list. It looked long, but none of the jobs were very big.

> To-Do List
>
> Pick up the things under your bed.
>
> Put your socks into the hamper.
>
> Hang up your pants.
>
> Put your dishes in the sink.
>
> Go to Mrs. Blum's shop and get 2 black pens and a lunchbox that will fit in your backpack.

"This will be quick!" he said. Ben picked up his pants and socks from under his bed. He hung up his pants and put his socks in the hamper, just as his mom had asked.

One by one, Ben put a check next to the jobs as he did them. His plan was to go pick up his school things and then go to Nick's. He put the cash in his pocket and left for Mrs. Blum's shop.

A bunch of kids were in Mrs. Blum's shop to get things for school. Ben was not in a rush. The shop had lots of things to look at.

At last Mrs. Blum was done helping the kids, so she asked Ben if he wanted help. She helped him get the things that were on his list and put them in a bag.

Mrs. Blum had a bucket of pens that were back-to-school gifts for the kids. She let Ben pick the one he wanted. He picked a black and silver pen.

"Thanks so much for the gift!" said Ben. "I've got

to go. My mom will be back at one."

He had done all the things on his to-do list, but he had one thing left to do. "After I put the bag on my desk, I will ask Mom if I can go to Nick's," he said. Ben felt happy. Summer was done and his best pal Nick was back.

Ms.

6

Ben was up at six o'clock. He put on his black pants, a top, and his good-luck socks.

He was in a rush to get to school. He wanted to see who was going to be in his class. What if Nick was not in his class? He packed his lunch and put his lunchbox in his backpack.

"There you are!" said Mrs. Hopkins. "You packed your lunch all by yourself? Well done! Sit and have a muffin. I'll get you a glass of milk," she said.

"Mom, I can't sit! I have to get to school!"

"Ben, there is no one at school yet," said Mrs. Hopkins. "After you have your muffin and milk, we'll go."

Ben got to school just as Mr. Hunter let the kids in. Mrs. Hopkins asked Ben to give her a big hug and a kiss. "Have a good day!" she said.

Mr. Hunter had all the class lists. He sent Ben to Ms. Block's class. Lots of kids said that Ms. Block's class was the best one and that it was fun. Ben met Ms. Block as she was helping kids put things into lockers.

Ben was looking for Nick, but he did not see him. As Ben was filling his locker, Justin bumped into him.

Ben's books fell, but Justin did not help him pick them up. Ben said to himself, "I don't think I am going to like Justin. I won't be happy if he is in my class."

As Ben went into his class, Justin passed by. "Justin is in my class," Ben said. "So much for my good-luck socks."

But then, Ben felt a tap on his back. There were Liz and Nick! They were going to be in Ms. Block's class. Ben was so happy to have Liz and Nick in his class. It looked like his socks were good-luck after all!

7

Ms. Block set up the chart of class helpers. There were lots of jobs on the chart. One boy had to put lunches in the lunch bin. Justin was going to look after the plants. Liz was glad that she got the job of tending to the class mascot, Marvin. Marvin was a black rabbit.

But Ben had the best job of all. Ms. Block asked him to look after the books in the class. It was not a hard job. He just had to pick up books at the end of the day and put them back on the shelf.

At the end of the day, Ben went from desk to desk to get all the books. He had so much fun doing his job. He put the big books on the bottom shelf and the rest on the top shelf.

"Thank you," Ms. Block said. "The bookshelf looks much better! You can pick a book for yourself, if you like."

It was hard for Ben to pick just one. There were lots of good books. At last, he plucked a thick book from the bottom shelf. "Is this a good one?" he asked Ms. Block.

"*The Big Book of Mars*," she said. "Yes, that is a good book. You'll have to tell me what you think after you read it."

Ben was happy as he got onto the bus that day. He clutched the book to his chest and said, "I am glad I had my good-luck socks on today. I got the best class job of all."

8

The next day after lunch, some of the kids went to the blacktop in back of the school. They were going to set up a basketball match. Nick and Ben like basketball so they went to help.

Ben forgot to put his reading glasses in his desk. He had them in the pocket of his jacket. "I better not slip and fall with my glasses in my pocket," he said. There were benches next to the blacktop, so Ben set his glasses there.

Nick was very good at basketball. He ran fast and was a good shot. A kid passed the ball to him and he darted on the blacktop from end-to-end.

Some of the kids said, "Go, Nick! Slam it in!" He jumped up to the basket and dunked the ball into the net. A slam dunk!

Next, Nick passed the ball to Ben. Ben ran to the basket, jumped up, and tossed the ball. The ball hit the rim of the basket and he missed the shot. The ball landed next to Justin who was on a bench looking at the match. He picked up the ball and tossed it back to Nick.

It was a good match and the kids had fun. Then the bell rang so the match ended. The kids had to go back to class. Ben went to get his glasses from the bench.

He picked up the glasses. One of the arms was bent. Ben was upset as he left for class.

"My glasses are busted. I just got my glasses and someone sat on them. The glasses will be hard to fix. My mom is not going to be happy," Ben said to himself.

"Justin was on the bench next to my glasses. What if he had bent the glasses?" Ben said. "I think that Justin is going to be hard to like."

(pumpkin)

9

One fall day the wind did not let up. Ben put on his thickest jacket and left for school. There was a chill, and it felt a bit like winter. Ms. Block had said that today she had something fun for the class to see.

The kids were all in class, but Ms. Block was not. That was odd. All of a sudden, there was Ms. Block with a plump pumpkin in her arms.

The pumpkin was so big that she did not see her desk. She bumped into it and said, "Help! Come quick! The pumpkin is going to fall!" Some kids jumped up and helped her lift the pumpkin onto her desk.

The pumpkin looked good. "I think this is my best class pumpkin yet," said Ms. Block. "Let's ask Mr. Hunter to come by and see it."

Ms. Block said, "I went to a pumpkin patch with my husband. We asked for the plumpest pumpkin they had. It was hard to get it to my car! Then my husband and I had to get it into my backyard."

"It was a big job to carve the pumpkin. The top was as hard as a rock, so I had to get something very sharp. Doing the top was by far the hardest part of the job. After I was done, I put some pumpkin, butter, and eggs in my blender and fixed muffins for all of us!"

"Thank you!" said the kids. The kids looked at the pumpkin for the rest of the day. And the pumpkin looked back at them.

10

Art class was one of the best classes at Chester School. Mr. Flanders had lots of fun things for the kids to do. Today Mr. Flanders was reading to the class from a book on bats.

"Bats can fly and see in the dark," said Mr. Flanders. "All bats have sharp fangs. They become active at dusk and they can catch insects as they fly."

After reading the book, Mr. Flanders flung it on his desk. He went to his cart and got some black felt and silver glitter. "You are going to cut up the felt to look like bats. After you cut the felt, you will add flecks of this glitter to the wings. By the end of class, you'll have a flying bat to hang up," said Mr. Flanders. "Look at me so you can do what I do."

Ben sat at his desk. He was not the fastest in art, but he was good at it. It was one of the best parts of his day. Last summer, he did a lot of art all by himself.

Some of the kids who sat next to Ben asked him for help with the wings. It was not hard for them to cut the felt. Adding the flecks of glitter was the hardest part of the job. The kids were adding globs of glitter, not flecks. That was not going to look good, so Ben helped them put on the glitter.

Liz did not like what her bat looked like. "I think this thing looks like a big black butterfly, not a bat," she said as she flung it on her desk.

Mr. Flanders sat next to her. He said, "Liz, I must admit that a black butterfly is not common, but this butterfly is very charming, and it will fly as well as the bats. Just add lots of glitter. It will be the best butterfly in the class." Liz felt better as she added some glitter.

"If you are done with your bats, put up your hand. I will come by and give you some yarn. Then you can hang up your bat," said Mr. Flanders. "Your bat will look like it can flap its wings and fly."

"Thanks, Mr. Flanders!" said the kids as they left art class with bats… and one butterfly in hand.

Thanksgiving

"

There was no school today. It was Thanksgiving! Ben and his mom were up with the sun. They were going to Nick's for a big Thanksgiving dinner.

Mrs. Hopkins had fixed some of her best dishes. There were platters of plum tarts and pumpkin muffins. Ben helped her pack them into bags. He sniffed and said, "Yum! Something smells good. Can I have a tart?"

"Not yet!" said Mrs. Hopkins. "We're going to have a big dinner at Nick's. No snacking until then." Ben and his mom packed the car and went to Nick's.

Mrs. Hopkins rang the bell. Mr. Foss, Nick's dad, let them in. "Happy Thanksgiving!" he said. "We are so glad to have you with us for dinner!"

Mrs. Hopkins handed Nick's mom one bag and said, "We are glad you asked us to come. Something smells good! What can we help you with?"

Nick's mom said, "The dishes are set. All that's left to do is fix the mashed yams. The boys can do that. Boys, you have to mash them well so that there are no lumps left in them."

"OK," they said. Mrs. Foss handed them a list of what to do with the yams.

Mashed Yams

1. Mash six big yams.
2. Melt 1/2 cup butter and mix with one cup of milk.
3. Add butter and milk to the yams.
4. Top with nuts.

Mashing the yams was a big job. They mashed them until no lumps were left. After they were done, Nick snuck a bit from the dish with his finger. "Shh! Don't snitch," he said to Ben.

"I won't!" said Ben. "Let me have some."

At last, they sat for dinner. As they all held hands, Nick's dad said, "This is a day to give thanks. We give thanks for good dishes and good pals to have them with. Happy Thanksgiving to you all! Let's dig in."

Winter

cold

12

It was a cold winter day. Ben was snug under his blankets and did not want to get up from bed. The sun was not up yet, so it was very dark. It was hard to get up for school in the winter. He wanted to spend the day in bed.

Ben was thinking that things were not going well with Nick. "I think Nick likes Justin a lot. What if Nick likes him better than me?" Ben said to himself.

"Ben!" Mrs. Hopkins said with a yell. "Get going. You don't want to miss the bus."

Ben jumped up. "Miss the bus?" he said. He looked at the clock and gasped. He snatched his flannel top and his thickest socks. He ran to his mom with one sock on and one in his hand.

She looked at him in shock and said, "Ben! Did you just get up? Good thing I packed your lunch for you! Get your jacket on, and I'll get your backpack."

"You'll have to have your muffin on the bus," she said as she handed him a muffin and a napkin. "And good luck on your spelling test today."

"Thanks, Mom!" said Ben. He sped to the bus. He got to the end of the block, but the bus was not there. "Did I miss it?" Ben was huffing and puffing and thinking of what to do next.

All of a sudden, there was a honk. Ben looked up. He was in luck. There was his bus! Ben darted to the bus and got on. There was a spot next to Liz, so he slid into it.

As the bus sped up, he felt much better. "I slept in and had to rush," he said to Liz. "I'm just so glad I didn't miss the bus."

"Your muffin smells so good," Liz hinted.

"This is one of my mom's pumpkin muffins. You can have some," Ben said as he split the muffin for them.

13

The next day Ms. Block was absent. Someone said she had the flu. Mr. Ford was going to be the sub for her class until she felt better. Mr. Ford was short and slim. He had on dark tan slacks and plastic glasses that were silver, just like Ben's.

Mr. Ford set his bag and his mug on Ms. Block's desk. He looked at the kids. "I'm Mr. Ford," he said. He held the class list in his hand and checked to see who was there and who was absent. "You'll have to forgive me if I forget who you are. There are a lot of you and just one of me."

"Let's see," he said. "I think we have to do some reading." The kids helped Mr. Ford get the books from the shelf. They sat and looked at Mr. Ford.

"What chapter are you on?" he asked. Mr. Ford marched back and forth as he looked in Ms. Block's plan book. "Hmm... Forget reading. Let's do spelling."

As he went to sit on Ms. Block's desk, Mr. Ford's back hit his mug. It splashed on the books that were on the desk! It splashed on his slacks! It fell and smashed into bits!

"My, my!" he said. "What a mess! I'll get to that in a bit. On with the spelling lesson!"

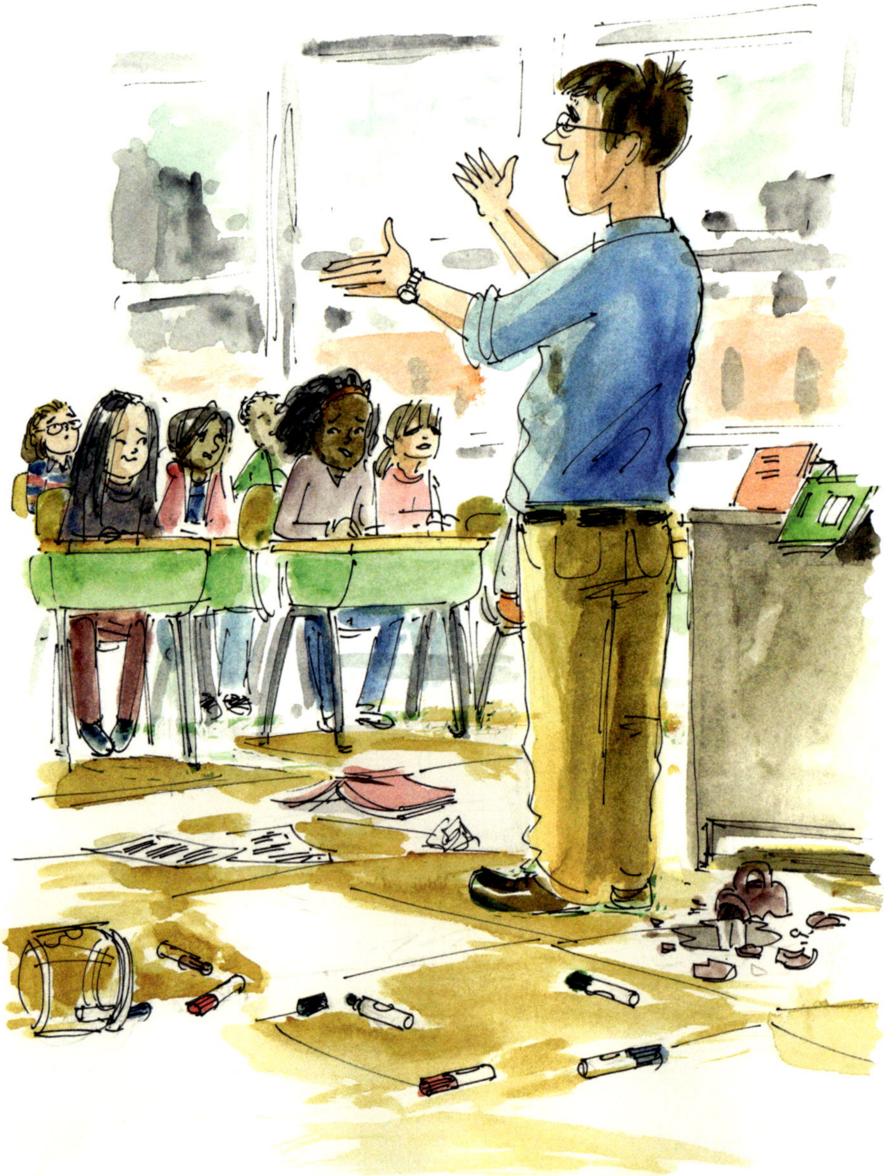

He was reading from Ms. Block's lesson plan as he went to get a marker from the plastic bin. He was not looking as he put his hand in the bin and it fell from the shelf. Markers went flying!

Some of the kids got up to help, but Mr. Ford said, "No, no! Forget the markers. We can pick them up in a bit. On with the spelling lesson!"

The rest of the day did not go much better. Mr. Ford forgot to let the kids have snacks at ten o'clock. He forgot to send them to art class. By the end of the day, the class was a mess.

As the bell rang, Mr. Ford looked at the kids. "Well, we did it. What a day! Do you think Ms. Block will forgive me for all this mess?" None of the kids said a thing. They were thinking that they wanted Ms. Block to get well fast… very fast.

14

At last Ms. Block was back at school. The kids were so glad to see her. This morning they were doing a math lesson on adding numbers. "For the next part of the lesson, pick someone to sit with. Then I will tell you what to do," Ms. Block said.

The kids got up and sat next to a pal. Ben went to Nick's desk to sit with him. Just as he got there, Nick got up. "Ben," he said, "I wanted to sit with you, but Justin just asked me to sit with him."

Ben said it was OK, but he felt glum. He looked up to see who was left. No one was. Ms. Block said, "Ben, you can go sit with Liz and Jess."

After all the kids had a pal to sit with, Ms. Block put packs of flash cards on the desks. She said, "This task will help you get faster with your math facts. If you can get faster with facts, you will be better at math. Mix the cards so that they are not in order."

The kids had to flip the cards and then add the numbers. Ms. Block marked on a chart who did the sums the fastest.

Ben had fun with Liz, and they were very good at the task. Liz was the smartest kid in the math class. She had shortcuts to get the sums.

She said, "If 8 + 8 is 16, then 8 + 7 will be one less. 8 + 7 = 15!"

But Ben was not thinking of adding numbers. He kept thinking of Nick and Justin. He was sort of upset that Nick was doing the math with Justin and not with him.

"Justin likes Nick, but I don't think Justin likes me at all," he said to himself. "I don't think that Justin and I will be pals."

After math class, the kids went to lunch. Nick sat with Ben. Ben forgot that he was upset. He was glad to be back with his best pal.

(snow)

15

The next morning Ms. Block put a chart up on the wall. It was a list of all the after-school clubs and sports. There were a lot to pick from. She asked the kids to tell her if they wanted to be in a club or do a sport.

Some of the kids picked the chess club, the math club, or the ping-pong club. Some picked the art club or the band. After the kids picked, Ms. Block marked the chart.

Ben was going to pick the book club. He spent a

lot of his days reading, and Ms. Block had a lot of books on her shelf. But there were a lot that he had not picked yet. He wanted to be in the book club and read all the books Ms. Block had.

After Ms. Block marked the chart, Ben asked Nick if he wanted to be in the book club with him. Nick said he did not. He wanted to do sports. Nick was tall and very good at basketball. He was going to do basketball with Justin.

The next day, the book club met after school. There were six kids in the club. Ms. Block said they did not have to sit at desks, so they sat on a small rug in the corner.

Ms. Block had picked a *Cam Jansen* book. "*Cam Jansen* books are a lot of fun! The good thing is that there are a lot of them. If you like this one, we will plan to also read the next one," she said.

By the end of the book club, all the kids were *Cam Jansen* fans. Ben put the book in his backpack and ran into the hall. He was happy as he left school. He had fun at the book club and it looked like it was going to snow!

16

The next day it started to snow in the morning. The kids were in school and the snow was falling faster and harder. Blasts of wind tossed the snow back and forth. It was going to be some big snowstorm!

Ms. Block went on with her lessons, but the kids just kept looking at the snow. They were thinking of all the fun things that they were going to do after school in the snow.

By ten o'clock, it was still snowing. There was a

thick blanket of snow on the blacktop. Ms. Block had to stop her lessons. The class was standing with Ms. Block looking at the snow.

"This snowstorm is bad," she said. "I didn't think it was going to snow this hard. It looks as if we have six inches, and it's still snowing!"

After music, the kids went back to Ms. Block's class. She said "Kids, school will end at one o'clock today. If the snow is very bad, the buses can't run. Let's all get packed up and I'll read you a short story until the bell rings."

Gusts of wind stung the kids as they went to the buses. The snow was thick, and it was hard to see. The cars were at a standstill. "What if the bus gets stuck?" Ben asked.

The man who ran the bus said to the kids, "It's going to be a long one! The bus can't go very fast in snow like this. If you sit still and put on your belts, we can get started."

"Do you think we will get a day off?" asked Liz.

Ben and his pals had lots of plans for what they were going to do if they had a snow day the next day.

17

The next morning it was still snowing. Ben got up at seven o'clock and it was very dark. He jumped up and picked up his backpack.

His mom looked in and said, "Ben, you can go back to bed. The storm looks like it's never letting up. You have a snow day."

Ben said, "No school!"

Ben was thinking of all the things he wanted to do with Nick that day. He and Nick spent snow days at the park. After a snowstorm, they went sledding or stacked snow for a fort.

Ben did not get back in bed. He wanted to get to Nick's fast. Ben did not have far to go, just seven blocks over. "What's on the menu this morning?" he asked his mom.

"Bacon and eggs," she said.

"Super!" said Ben. He finished his bacon and eggs as quick as a wink. "I'm going to go over to the park with Nick."

"OK. You can go after you finish your milk," said Mrs. Hopkins. "Be back by one o'clock."

The snowstorm was still not over. It was snowing

hard. None of the shops were open, and the cars were snowed in. It was hard to see the path to Nick's under the thick blanket of snow.

The snow was wet and thick. It was up to the top of Ben's legs. It was getting hard for him to pick up his legs. At last, he got to Nick's.

Nick's dad let Ben in. He said, "You just missed Nick. He and Justin left for the park. Run as fast as you can and you will catch up with them."

"It's hard to go fast in this snow," said Ben. "I won't catch up."

Ben was shocked that Nick had left for the park and had not asked him to go. He had just asked Justin. Going to the park after snowstorms was something he and Nick did. He was sad that Nick and Justin had become such good pals.

Ben started walking to the park. It was snowing.

18

The kids from school met in the park with sleds. It was cold, but they had put on thick jackets and mittens. They were happy as they slid in the soft snow. One by one, they went up to the top of the hill with sleds and slid to the bottom.

Some of the kids began to form the snow into big balls. They stacked the balls into a snowman. One of the boys put his scarf on the snowman's neck. Next, they put in sticks for arms. The snowman did not look like a human being. Still, the kids felt that the snowman was super.

Ben got to the park and started looking for Nick. Nick and a bunch of kids were stacking snow for a fort. Nick looked up. "Ben! Ben!" he said. "Come help us!" Ben ran over and started packing snow on the fort. He was happy that Justin was not with Nick.

As they were finishing up, Ben felt a snowball land on his back. The next moment, all the kids began flinging snowballs back and forth. Nick and Ben began to pack the snow into balls faster and faster.

They ducked as the snowballs landed next to them and on top of them. Some of the snowballs were big and some were small. The kids had so much fun.

The next moment Justin yelled, "Ben!" Ben looked up just as Justin pitched a snowball at him. Ben got hit hard.

This snowball was as hard as a rock. The cold snow stung Ben's chin. Ben felt his chin with his mitten. His chin was cut.

Justin ran off. Ben was so mad at him. Ben didn't want his pals to see that he was upset, so he left the park. The fun was over for him.

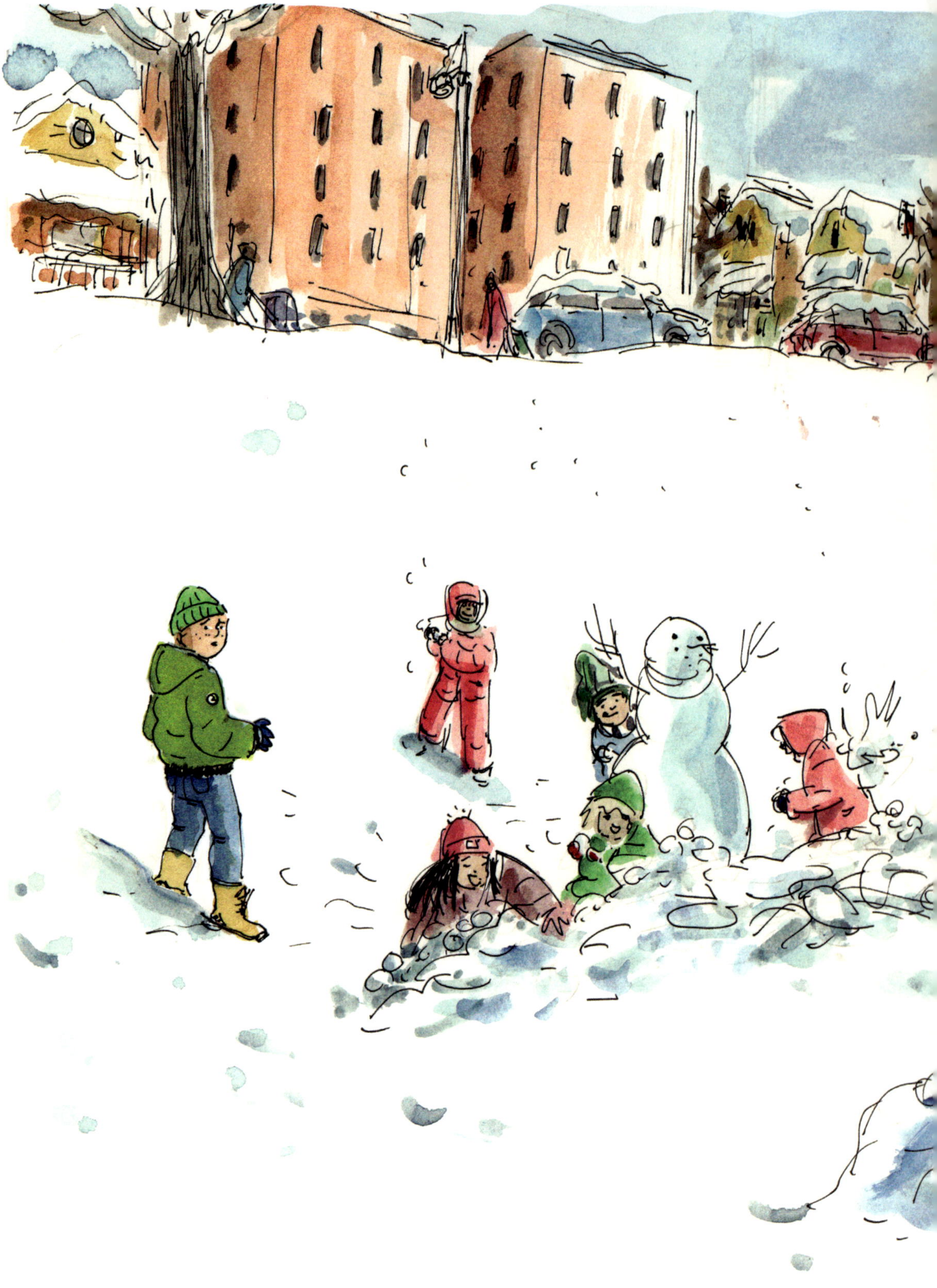

67

19

From the moment Ben got up, he felt sick. His neck was stiff and he was stuffed up. As he was packing his lunch, his mom said, "You don't look well. I don't think you can go to school today."

"I have book club with Ms. Block after school," said Ben with a sniff. "I don't want to miss it!"

"I'm glad you want to go to school, but I can't send you if you are sick. You will get the rest of the kids sick. Let's visit the clinic and see what Dr. Martin thinks," she said.

Mrs. Hopkins called Chester School to tell them that Ben was going to be absent that day. She also called her job to tell them Ben was ill so she was not going to be in.

Then, Ben and his mom went to the clinic. The parking lot was packed. The clinic was filled with sick kids. Some were standing and some were sitting. They all looked as if they belonged in bed.

At last, Ben was called in to see Dr. Martin. She checked Ben's lungs and also felt to see if he was hot. "It looks like you have a fever," she began. "This isn't just a cold. I think you have the flu. Lots of kids are getting the flu this winter. You must rest in bed until you are better."

Just as Ben and his mom got back from the clinic,

Nick ran up to them with a big get well card in his hand.

Nick said to Ben, "I can't come in. I don't want to catch the flu. I just wanted to give this to you. We all missed you at school today."

Nick handed Ben the card, and he opened it. All the students in Ms. Block's class had added something to the card, even Justin.

"Tell the kids thank you," said Ben. Ben relaxed in bed and slept for the rest of the day. After getting the card and his long nap, he felt much better.

20

Ben was back at school. He was skipping up the steps and into his class, happy to be with his pals. Ms. Block said, "Good to see you. We missed you."

Ms. Block began reading a book to the class on the sun and the planets. "The sun is a star," she began. "And a star is a big ball of gas in the sky. There are 8 planets that orbit the sun."

"Some planets are big and some are small. Some planets are hot and some are cold. The coldest planets are the ones far from the sun."

"We are going to see a short film on the planets. After the film, you will do a report on the planet that you pick. You will have seven days to finish your report."

Ben jumped up and yelled, "Ms. Block! Ms. Block! Can I have Mars? I just finished the book on Mars. Mars has lots of red dust, so it is called the Red Planet. We have sent rovers to see if humans can live there. Rovers are like robot cars and…"

"Relax, Ben," said Ms. Block. "We are all going to see the film, and then we will pick planets for the reports."

Ben did not have to see the film to pick a planet. He had spent his days off from school finishing his book on Mars. "I will start my report after school today. What a good day to come back!" he said.

21

Seven days after the snowstorm there was still snow on the cars and paths. Some of the kids in Ben's class went to school on the bus and some walked. Nick and Ben walked in the fall, but in the winter they went on the bus. They did not like walking in the cold.

That day, Ben had missed his bus and was walking to school by himself. He was swinging his arms and humming a song. As he got to the corner, he spotted Mrs. Mendez walking her dog. The dog's legs were very short, so it was hard for him to walk in the snow.

Ben said, "Good morning, Mrs. Mendez."

"Good morning, Ben," she said.

Mrs. Mendez was not happy. She had on her winter jacket and a long black scarf, yet she was still shivering. The skin on her hands was very red. "Did you forget your mittens?" asked Ben.

She put her hands into her jacket pockets and got the mittens. "I was rushing to get going on my walk. I didn't forget my mittens. They are in my jacket pockets. I just forgot to put them on!" said Mrs. Mendez.

"Well, if you put them on your hands, you won't be so cold," Ben said.

"I will," said Mrs. Mendez as she started walking to the corner. "It was swell talking to you."

Ben walked past the bookshop and the barbershop. Some shops had still not opened after the storm. He walked past the supermarket. It was open, but no one was in the market yet.

As he got to school, Ben looked up at the sky. He said to himself, "It looks as if it will snow today. That will be super! This is going to be such a swell day."

22

Ben was spending his days off doing odd jobs. He had put up an ad in the market and was starting to get a lot of calls.

Want a good helper?
Shopping
Dog walking
Pet sitting
Odd jobs

Call Ben
555-1945

After school, he walked one of the dogs from his block. It was a lot of fun, but he did not like picking up after him. On some days Nick walked to the park with Ben, and they tossed a tennis ball back and forth for the dog.

Ben also helped Mr. Clinton. It was hard for Mr. Clinton to walk. Ben went with him to the market and helped him do his shopping. Ben also helped look after Mr. Clinton's plants.

Some days Ben's job was just sitting and talking with Mr. Clinton. Mr. Clinton was happy to have Ben helping him, but he was also happy to have someone to talk to.

One day snow began falling. It was not as bad as the last snowstorm, but it was still a mess. Some of the parked cars were stuck.

Ms. Martin swept snow from the top of her car as Ben walked by. "I can't even see your car under all that snow," Ben said. "Can I help you?"

"My car is sitting under ten inches of snow from the last storm," said Ms. Martin. "I'll be glad to get some help."

Ben and Ms. Martin dug and dug until there was no snow left on the car. As she got in, she thanked him and handed him some cash. "You didn't have to help me and you did such a good job. Thank you," she said.

"Thank you," he said. "I'm happy to help!"

Ben was glad that he had helped Ms. Martin and

was happy to have some cash to add to his stash. He kept a box under his bed with all the cash. It was starting to fill up!

Spring

(spring)

23

Spring had come and the long winter was over. Ben and his class were going to visit Aspen Garden. Aspen Garden was a plot of land that belonged to the school. The students got to go to the garden in the fall and in the spring. Today, the class was going to have a gardening lesson.

Ben was happy not to have to sit at a desk all day. He had tended to Mr. Clinton's plants, but never a big garden. Ms. Block said all the kids were going to get to plant something.

Ms. Jackson was standing by the garden. She was a master gardener. She was going to give the lesson on gardening.

"Good morning kids," said Ms. Jackson. "We will start by going on a garden walk. What a splendid day we have! The starlings are singing for you. And look at that butterfly flapping its black and red wings!"

"Where? Where is the butterfly?" asked Jess. "I cannot see it." The butterfly had vanished.

The students walked in the garden and looked at all the plants and even the insects. Also, there were some spiders spinning webs in the garden. Ms. Jackson said spiders were good for the plants.

Next, the class went to see the beds where they

had planted tulip bulbs in the fall. The tulips were just starting to blossom. Twelve of the bulbs were going to be dark pink tulips, and twelve were going to be red.

"You must come back and see the tulips after the buds have opened. The tulips are splendid!" said Ms. Jackson.

Ms. Jackson helped the kids plant corn, peppers, and yams. "They have to have lots of sun," she said. They also helped to clip back some of the plants that were very big.

As they were walking to the exit, Liz spotted something and asked, "Ms. Jackson, what is this?" Ms. Jackson and all the students went over to where Liz was standing. Liz was next to a nest

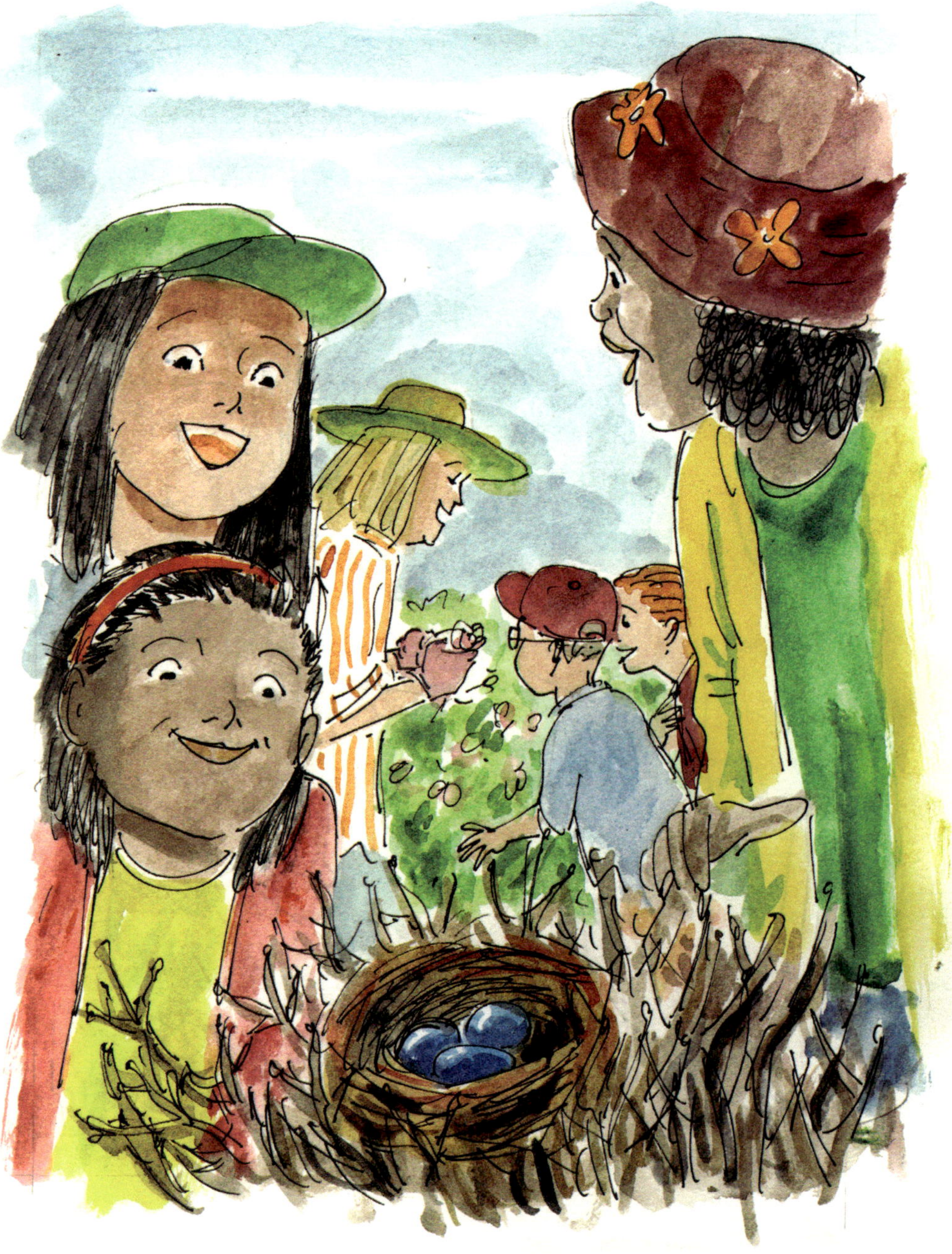

of small twigs and grass. There were some eggs in the nest.

"Look kids," said Ms. Jackson. "This nest belongs to a robin. Robins are very common in the spring. I'm glad we got to see it."

Ms. Block said, "It's twelve o'clock. We better get back to school for lunch. Let's thank Ms. Jackson for a super gardening lesson." The class thanked her. Then they left the garden and started walking back to school.

"Can we come back to see the robins after they hatch?" asked one of the boys.

"I'll do my best," said Ms. Block. "We have to ask Mr. Hunter if it is OK for the class to come back. But we did get to see robin's eggs today!"

24

There was a lot of traffic. Trucks and cars were honking as the class went back to school. At last, the bus got there.

Mr. Hunter was walking back and forth on the school steps looking for them. "Where were you?" he asked Ms. Block. "Did you get lost?"

Ms. Block said, "No. We were not lost. There was just so much traffic."

"Did you get a lot done at the garden?" Mr.

Hunter asked.

"Yes," said Ms. Block. "We did some planting and looked at the tulips that were planted last fall. We got to see a robin's nest. The trip to the garden was super, but I think we better go have some lunch."

"OK," said Mr. Hunter. "Let's all go in."

After lunch Ms. Block wanted the class to have a rest. "This morning, there were some spiders in the garden. I am going to read a chapter in this book called *Super Spiders*," and she started to read.

★ ★ ★

Do you like spiders or do you run if you see one? Spiders are not as bad as you think. There are all sorts of spiders.

Common spiders like to live in dark spots such as under steps and rocks. They spin silk webs to try to trap insects. They have fangs with venom that kills the insects.

Spiders also spin egg sacs. The eggs are in the sacs until the spiders hatch. The silk strands they spin are very, very strong.

Do you think spiders are insects? They are not. Insects have six legs and wings. Spiders do not have six legs and do not have wings.

Common spiders will not harm human beings. In fact, spiders are a big help to the plants in gardens. They catch the insects that harm the plants. All in all, spiders are splendid!

25

Ben likes doing his small jobs. He also likes basketball and doing arts and crafts. But best of all, Ben likes reading his comic books. His comics are stashed in a trunk at the end of his bed.

He had some Batman and Superman books, but no Spider-Man comics. Some of the kids said Spider-Man was the strongest super hero and the best comic book. Ben wished he had one.

One day after school, Ben and his mom went to the bookshop. Ben still had some cash from the odd jobs he had done over the winter.

At the shop, all the comics were stacked on the far wall. Ben walked over to the bookshelf. There were twelve Spider-Man books! He wanted to get them all, but he had to pick just one. He picked the one that looked like Spider-Man was falling from the sky.

The next morning, Ben wanted to read his comic on the bus, so he packed it in his backpack. Then at school Ben put it in his locker. He put it on top of his lunch, so it did not get crushed.

"I'll come back after music and get it," Ben was thinking to himself. "I bet Nick will want to see it at lunch." Justin walked by just as Ben was stashing his stuff in his locker.

After music class, Ben walked back to his locker and was shocked to see that it was open. He said, "That's odd. I don't think I left my locker open." Ben looked into his locker. The Spider-Man comic book had vanished!

Ben was trying not to cry. He did not want the kids to see him crying, so he ducked into Mr. Smith's class. No one was there.

Ben was mad at himself. It was not smart of him to have left the comic book in his locker. What if it was lost forever? Did Justin see him put the comic in his locker? Had Justin opened his locker? Did Justin have his comic?

26

Ben went back to his class. He was still upset that he had lost his comic book. Ms. Block was going to read a story to the kids. "This is a short story called *The North Wind and The Sun*. The story has a lesson. After I finish reading, I'm going to ask you to tell me what you think the lesson is," she said.

One day the North Wind and the Sun had a chat. "I am much stronger than you are," said the Wind.

"I don't think so," said the Sun.

"I am," said the Wind. "Let's have a contest and see who is stronger. You see that man walking over there? I bet I can get his jacket off him faster than you can."

"I don't think so," said the Sun, "But I will let you try."

The North Wind was thinking to himself, "I will get that jacket off with one good gust of wind. It won't be hard to do."

So the North Wind started huffing and puffing. He blasted a strong gust of wind. He blasted so hard that robins fell from the sky. He blasted so hard that the man had dust all over him.

But no matter what the North Wind did, the jacket did not come off the man. The shivering man clung to his jacket. The sad Wind said, "I am done. I give up. I cannot blast that jacket off."

The Sun wanted to try. Up, up he went until he filled the sky. But he was not harsh like the North Wind. The Sun was tender.

The Sun got just a bit hotter and the man tugged at his jacket. The Sun got hotter and the man opened his jacket. But he still had the jacket on. So at last, the Sun got still hotter until the man was sweltering. He had to get his jacket off.

"What did you do to get the jacket off?" asked the North Wind.

"I just lit the day up," said the Sun with a grin.

———————————

Ms. Block shut her book and asked, "Who wins the contest in the end, the Wind or the Sun?"

Nick put his hand up and said, "The Sun was the winner."

"Good," said Ms. Block. She looked at the kids and called on Ben. "Ben, what do you think the lesson of this story is?"

Ben was not thinking of the story. He was still thinking of Justin and the comic book. "I think the lesson is that hot things are stronger than cold things," he said. Ms. Block did not look happy. Ben said to himself, "This is not the best day I have ever had."

Then Liz's hand shot up and she said, "I think the lesson is that being clever can be better than just being strong."

"Splendid!" said Ms. Block just as the lunch bell clanged.

27

It was a splendid spring day. Ben and Nick had plans after school. They were going to go to the park to have a basketball match.

There were lots of kids at the park. Ben went over to the blacktop. Nick was not there yet. Ben picked up a basketball and began tossing it. After what felt like forever, he said, "Where is Nick? I just talked with him at lunch. It's not like him to forget."

Ben tossed the ball a bit longer and then he called

it quits. He did not think Nick was going to come after all, and he had to get back for dinner. He was upset as he walked back by himself.

His mom was frying soft shell crabs. Yum. They smelled super. She yelled, "Hi, Ben! Put your backpack in the closet, and come help me with dinner."

Ben walked up to his mom. "What's the matter?" she asked. "You look so glum."

Ben had a talk with his mom. "Don't be cross with Nick," she said. "He's your best friend. Just give him a call and ask him what happened."

Ben sat on his bed and called Nick. Nick picked up after one ring. "Hi, Ben!" he said. "What's up?"

Ben was sitting very still and trying not to cry. He asked, "Where were you today? I was at the park after school. We had plans. What happened?"

Nick was silent. Then he said, "Ben, I forgot that we had plans. I was at school."

Ben asked, "Were you with Justin?"

"Yes," said Nick. Ben was silent.

Nick said, "I just forgot. Can you forgive me?"

"Yes, but I missed you. I don't like that you spend your days with Justin and not me. I don't trust him. I think he's the one who snatched the comic book from my locker," Ben said.

"Justin is a good friend, but you are my best

friend. Let's have a basketball match on Sunday?" Nick asked. "I won't forget. OK?"

He felt better. Still, he did not trust Justin.

"OK," said Ben and he hung up.

28

The class was going to Aspen Garden to check on the plants they had planted with Ms. Jackson. Ms. Block said, "The bus will drop us off at the garden. After we visit the garden, we will walk to the park for a picnic. Pack your lunches and have a drink. Then we will get going."

All the kids were happy and chatting as they packed up. All but Ben. He was still upset about his Spider-Man comic. He had looked all over the school! He had looked in the halls, in the classes, and in the bin of lost items. He had asked Mr. Franklin and Mr. Hunter. He had even looked in the desks in his class, but it was still missing. What bad luck!

As Ben was dragging his backpack to his desk, Justin walked over to him and handed him a comic book.

"What's this?" asked Ben. He looked at the comic book and gasped. His Spider-Man comic! It was back but the book was messed up.

Ben was mad. He yelled, "Where was it? Are you the one who opened my locker and snatched it?"

"No! I went to see Mr. Smith for math help and he asked me to drop my gum in the trash. Your comic book was there, sticking out of the trash can. Nick said you had lost one so I picked it up," Justin said.

"This was my best comic. Thank you, Justin!" said Ben. "Will you forgive me for thinking you were the one who opened my locker?"

"Yes. It's OK. Friends?" he asked.

"Friends," Ben said.

As Justin walked back to his desk, Ben was thinking, "Looks like Justin is someone I can trust after all."

29

The day of Justin's report was hard to forget. His topic was frogs. "Today I will tell you some frog facts," he said to the class. "I also have something for you to see." With a big grin, he lifted the top of a small box. In the box was his pet frog. He held the frog up for the class to see.

"This is Grover, my pet frog. I spotted him in some tall grass in the park," Justin said as he patted his frog. Justin did his report and then he let kids come up and pet Grover.

All of a sudden, the frog jumped from Justin's hand. It was hopping all over the class. "Grab him!" Justin yelled. The students rushed after Grover, but he was very fast.

A kid yelped and jumped up on his desk. "Get him!" he said. Grover jumped from desk to desk. As kids went to grab him, they bumped into stacks of books. Liz's lunchbox went flying and landed with a crash.

Then Grover jumped up onto Ms. Block's desk. Ms. Block went to grab Grover, but she lost her grip and the frog jumped off her desk. "He's so slick!" she yelled. "I can't catch him!"

"Look! Over there!" Justin said. He's on top of the chart!"

Ben ran to the chart. He had to jump over all the books. With one hand, Ben grasped the frog and put him back into the box. Justin shut the lid. "Thanks, Ben!" he said huffing. "You're a hero!"

Ms. Block and the kids began to get the class back in order. They put the books back on the shelf and the lunchbox back on Liz's desk. Ms. Block said, "Let's put a book on that lid, Justin."

"What a report!" she added with a grin.

30

The next day there was no school. Ben was going over to Nick's to have brunch with him and his mom and dad. Ben was bringing some fresh bran muffins.

He was also bringing some of his comic books. One of the comics was called *Dragon Masters*. Nick had asked if he could read that one. "You will like *Dragon Masters*," Ben had said to Nick. "It's a grand story!"

Justin was also at Nick's. Ben was not upset to

see Justin. He didn't think Justin was a brat at all. They had become good friends.

The boys had brunch and talked. Then they sat on Nick's steps looking at the comics. "What do you want to do next?" Justin asked.

"We can be dragon masters," said Ben.

"No," said Nick. "I don't like *Dragon Masters.*"

Justin said, "Well, I can get us a strong stick and a ball to set up a stickball match. Do you like stickball, Nick?"

Ben said, "I don't want to brag, but I am very good at stickball."

Nick said, "OK. Let's do it."

Justin got back with a stick and ball. The boys started the match. There was not a lot of traffic on Nick's block, so it was one of the best spots for stickball.

Some of the kids on the block ran over and asked to be in the match. There was a brisk wind that day, so the kids did not get hot. They all had a blast!

But just then, Nick looked up. His mom was on the steps calling to them. "You better come back in! Your moms and dads will be picking you up in a bit," she said.

"Not yet!" Ben called back to her.

"The match isn't over yet, Mom," Nick yelled. "Do we have to come in?"

"We're happy to have you boys. Let me call and check with your moms and dads," she said. After calling, Mrs. Foss went back to talk to the boys. They were in luck. They weren't going to be picked up yet. The stickball match did not have to end.

The boys dashed back to the match. At last, the kids on the block had to go. Ben, Nick, and Justin picked up the stick and ball and walked back to Nick's. As they walked, they talked of the match. They were happy to be friends.

31

In the spring all the kids at Chester School had testing. It was not fun. They had to read, spell, and do math problems. "Don't open your booklets until I tell you to begin," Ms. Block said as she passed the tests to her students.

Ms. Block set the clock. "After you finish part one, stop," she said. "Don't go on. Just be silent and let the rest of the class finish the test. Then I will let you all have a drink and a stretch."

Part one was math facts. Ms. Block said, "Start,"

and the students opened the booklets and began to do the test. The facts were not hard for Ben, but some of the students in his class looked stressed. Ms. Block said, "All I ask is that you try to do your best."

The second part of the test was math problems. The problems were harder for Ben. "I prefer to do math facts, not problems," he said to himself. "But I will try my best." By the end of the day, he was very glad that testing was over.

"You've had a long day," said Ms. Block after she picked up the tests. "You all did well and didn't give up. Let's have a stretch and a snack. I have some cold drinks and pretzels. If you prefer popcorn, I also have that."

"It won't be long until the bell rings, so I'll read

you a short story. "Justin, I think you'll like this story a lot," she said with a grin. "It's called *The Frog That Didn't Give Up.*"

One day a frog was jumping on a path and passed by a barn. She looked into the barn. No one was there. "I think I will go in and see what I can see," said the frog.

The barn was dark, but in jumped the frog. She landed on the rim of a bucket of fresh milk. There were drops of milk on the rim. Splash! The frog fell into the bucket.

The frog swam back and forth in the milk trying to get to the top of the bucket. Her legs were very strong, but it was hard to get up to the top. She stretched her long back legs to try to kick off from the bottom. No luck. The frog was stuck.

Still, she did not quit. She kicked her long legs harder and harder. Back and forth, the frog swam. She swam so fast that the bucket went from being a bucket of milk to being a bucket of butter!

The frog got up on top of the butter and jumped over the rim. She jumped back onto the path and said to herself, "Never give up!"

32

On Sunday Nick's mom and dad were bringing him and Ben to opening day at the ballpark. They were going to see the Mets and the Red Sox. Nick was a Mets fan and Ben was a Red Sox fan. The boys had on caps and mitts.

They walked to the bus. It was full of fans going to the ballpark, so they had to cram into the bus. Then someone yelled, "Let's go Mets!" Someone yelled back, "The Red Sox are the best!" All the fans started yelling back and forth in good fun.

There were lots of cars and buses traveling to the ballpark, so traffic was bad. Nick's mom said to him, "Don't forget to stick with Ben. The ballpark will be full of fans, and we don't want you to get lost. I'm going to give you your tickets. Put them in your pockets until we get there."

The ballpark was packed full. The boys walked until they got to the stands. "This is us!" Mrs. Foss said as she sat on a bench in the grandstand.

The kids sat and Nick's dad handed them snacks. They had pretzels and cold drinks. As they munched, someone from the Mets hit the ball with a full swing and it went flying into the grandstand.

Nick jumped up to try and catch it. It missed his

mitt by an inch. Plop! It landed in his mom's lap! "Good catch, Mom!" yelled Nick.

Just then, there was a crack of thunder and a sudden gust of wind. The kids looked up to see that the sky was black. The wind picked up and napkins and programs went flying. Even Ben's cap landed on the grass. And then the dark sky opened up.

"Don't panic!" yelled Nick's mom. "Let's go into the snack bar until the storm stops." The kids sprang up from the bench. They sprinted into the snack bar, splashing as they went. They were all drenched!

Nick and Ben started shivering, so they had hot drinks. They kept looking up at the sky, but the storm went on and on. At last, when it looked as if the storm was going to go on forever, the fans started to go.

Mr. Foss and the boys were glum. "We didn't get to see the Mets and the Red Sox for very long," said Ben.

"But what we did see was super," said Mrs. Foss with a grin. She was still clutching the ball and was thrilled to have it.

33

On the last day of school, the students jumped and yelled as the bell rang. They had spent the day packing up school things and being helpful to Ms. Block. The desks and lockers were spotless.

Ben left with an armful of books that Ms. Block was lending him for the summer. His backpack was stuffed with papers and sketches from art class.

Ben, Nick, and Justin were walking in the hall.

Kids ran by them, but the boys were in no rush. They were thankful that summer was starting. After the boys said "So long!" to Ms. Block and Mr. Hunter, they walked to the park. It felt good to be done with school.

At the park, the boys talked of the plans they had for summer. Nick was going back to camp and Justin was going with him. Ben was happy for his friends but wished that he was going to camp with them. Last summer he had missed being with Nick. With Justin going to camp also, there was going to be even less for Ben to do all summer.

Not long after the boys got to the park, Ben's mom got there to pick him up.

"Hi, boys!" she said.

"Hi, Mrs. Hopkins," they said.

She asked the boys what they were doing over the summer. Nick and Justin said they were going to camp. Mrs. Hopkins looked at Ben, who was very upset. She began to grin.

"Ben," she said. "I got a good call this morning after you left for school."

"Who called?" Ben asked.

"Someone from Camp Hilltop. I had called to ask if there were spots left for this summer. It looks like there is one spot left, and it's going to be yours," she said.

Ben was so happy. He jumped up to hug his mom. He was thankful that he was going to spend the summer with his friends.

Justin and Nick were yelling and clapping. They crushed Ben with a big hug.

The boys yelled, "We're ALL going to go to camp this summer!"

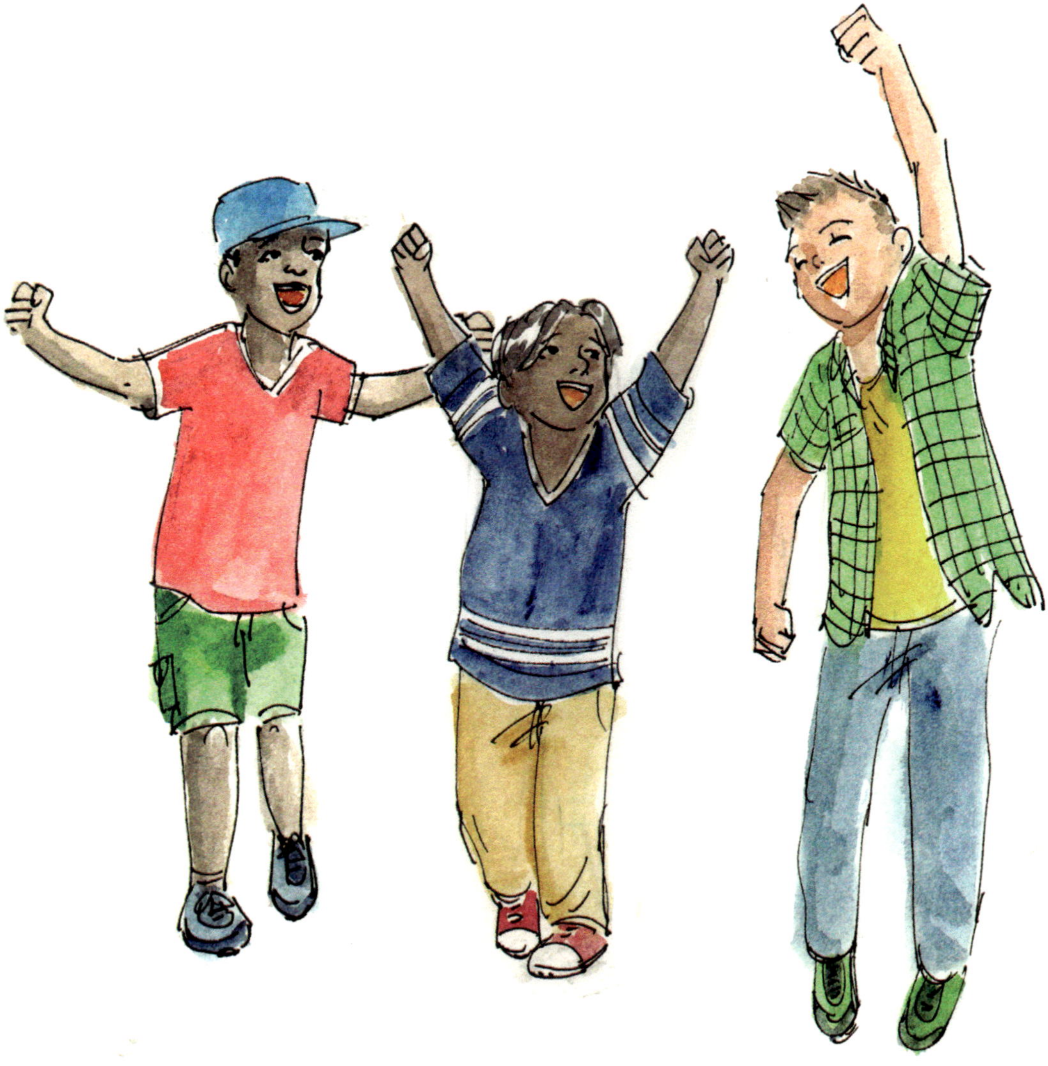

The *PAF Reading Series* provides decodable controlled text for beginning readers. *Decodable* means the words presented contain only letter sounds that children have been taught, so that they can sound out words. *Controlled* means that there is repetition in the vocabulary, allowing children to begin to recognize common words, with the length of words and sentences increasing gradually.

The Reading Series follows the instructional sequence in *PAF*, but it can be used to supplement any reading program. The level numbers in the upper right-hand corner of each title page refer to the corresponding level in the *PAF* program.

The words in ovals in the left-hand corner are phonetic words that contain elements not taught yet. Read the words in the ovals to the children before they read the story and tell them that it is a new word. Thereafter, anytime the children hesitate at an *oval* word, read it for them. The *oval* words are needed to provide coherent sentence structures.

The *oval* words that have been introduced prior to *Stand By Me* are: *all, ball, book, day, corn, for, good, happy, her, like, see, story, swim*.

The first three readers introduce the most common sound of each of the 26 letters of the alphabet in three-letter words.

Pals

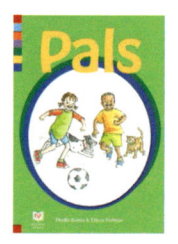

Consonants *b, c, d, f, g, h, j, l, m, n, p, r, s, t, v, y*, and the short vowel *a*
Suffix: *-s*
Nonphonetic Words: *the, to, you, your, said*

Fun In The Sun

Consonants *k, w, x, z, qu*, and the short vowels *i* and *u*
Nonphonetic Words: *of, are, they, put*

Let's Go

Short vowels *o* and *e*, and the digraphs *ch* and *th*
Suffixes: *-ing, -ed*
Compound Words
Nonphonetic Words: *was, from, were, very, do, goes*

Camp Hilltop

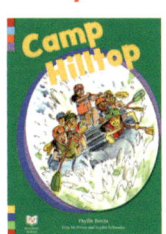

Digraph *sh* and Final Blends
Two-Syllable Root Words: VCCV *(rabbit)*
Suffixes: *-es, er*
Contractions
Nonphonetic Words: *don't, won't, who, school, want*

Stand By Me

Initial Blends and R-controlled Vowels *-ar* and *-or*
Two-Syllable Root Words: VCV *(robot)*
Suffixes: *-est, -ful, -less*
Nonphonetic Words: *one, done, none, what, there, some, come, off, walk, talk, where, friend, full*

Are We There Yet?

Common Long Vowels
Suffixes: *-en, -y, -ly*
Homonyms
Nonphonetic Words: *could, would, should, their, sure, says, does, only, again*

PAF is a comprehensive program for teaching reading, writing, and spelling in the primary grades using multisensory techniques. For more detailed information about multisensory reading instruction and the specific instructional techniques used in *PAF*, visit

pafprogram.com